The March

My mama and papa work very hard in the fields.

They pick grapes all day long. They have to be strong to do this kind of work. It's very hot out there in the fields.

At the end of the day, Mama and Papa are very tired. They have worked hard. But they don't get paid very much. Some growers care only about selling their grapes and making money.

One day, Mama and Papa learned about a great man. His name was Cesar Chavez. He was fighting for the rights of the grape pickers and farm workers. He didn't think the way they were treated was fair. He wanted them to make more money. He wanted their jobs to be safer and easier.

Mama and Papa became very excited. They wanted to go and see Mr. Chavez. They wanted to hear him speak. But they didn't have the time. They worked seven days a week in the fields. Still, they thought what he was doing was important. They hoped Mr. Chavez knew how they felt.

One morning, Mama said, "Papa, take Pedro and Marta. Today is the day. Go and meet Mr. Chavez. He is having a big march today. Tell him how much we like him. Let him know that we believe in what he is doing."

I was so excited. I was going to meet Mr. Chavez and march with him.

I rushed to get ready. I braided my hair and put on my best dress.

We said good-bye to Mama and set out on our journey.

We rode in a truck with other grape pickers to Delano. That's the town where the march was starting. It wasn't far. The farm where Mama and Papa pick grapes is nearby.

When we got there, a lot of people had gathered. It was still early. I shivered in my dress. Winter was over, but there was still a chill in the morning air.

"¡Hola!" another grape picker greeted Papa. Suddenly, everyone became quiet. Mr. Chavez was about to speak.

Papa listened closely as Mr. Chavez talked. All of the grape pickers listened to him attentively. I couldn't really hear him very well. Neither could Pedro. He poked me in the ribs and grinned.

Finally, it was time to march. Someone handed Papa the edge of a banner. The banner said "Viva La Causa." That means "Long Live Our Cause." I asked Papa to explain it to me.

"It means we will never give up, Marta," he replied. "We will fight until all farm workers have a better life."

I was proud of Papa for being so brave and carrying the banner. I held my head high and marched along beside him. Pedro held my hand and marched, too. We walked on the road that led out of Delano. We were headed to Sacramento, California's state capital.

HUELGA
NFWA
HUELGA
STRIKE
VIVA
LA CAUSA

"How far is it to Sacramento, Papa?" I asked.

"It's about 350 miles," he replied.

I must have looked worried, because Papa bent down to me. "What is it, chica?" he asked.

"Oh, Papa," I said, "I don't think I can walk 350 miles!"

Papa laughed and laughed, and Pedro laughed, too. I didn't know what was so funny!

"Oh, Marta," Papa explained, when he had stopped laughing. "We will not walk all the way to Sacramento. Your mama is expecting us at home tonight for dinner. We will walk only a little way. Then Felipe will give us a ride back to the farm. There are others who will continue the march for our cause."

That made me feel better. I began to march with my knees high. In my head I chanted, "March, march, march. March, march, march."

I kept my eyes on Mr. Chavez at the front. He looked like a kind and gentle man. I thought about how he was working to make Mama and Papa's lives easier.

I walked for almost an hour this way. Then the people in front stopped marching. I did, too. Pedro tapped me on the shoulder.

"It's time for us to go, Marta," he said.

I fell asleep in Papa's lap on the way home. When I woke up, I was in my house. Mama was putting dinner on the table.

"How was it, mi chica?" she asked.

I yawned and said sleepily, "It was very nice. Mr. Chavez is a great man. He will make our lives better. I just know it."